# "We don't wear pajamas at my house!"

"123 A to Z
enjoy these special memories"

Compiled by
Mrs. Boerma   Mrs. Eberhardt

Cover Art by
Danielle Fox

## ACKNOWLEDGMENTS

"We don't wear pajamas at my house!" represents 20 years of Athens Academy K-4 student quotes from the annually published "Famous Quotations". The comments, conversations and opinions conceived in 48-month-old minds reveal their innocence, honesty, curiosity, wisdom and insightfulness. This is one of the many enjoyments of teaching this age group. We get to experience this very important time in their lives as they figure out and piece together the world.

The title of the book was inspired by a quote delivered in response to the announcement of K-4 Pajama Day. It is one of the favorites, because after it appeared in our "Famous Quotations", we received four phone calls from parents asking if it was their child who had revealed the family secret!

The art on the pages of the book was accomplished by the Athens Academy K-4 students. Their ability to communicate through their drawings is quite evident. Please enjoy their work!

## DEDICATION

"We don't wear pajamas at my house!" is dedicated to Mr. Fred Bridges, Mrs. Diana Maxwell and Mrs. Nancy Robertson. Teaching is a team effort, and these were the constants on our team.

COPYRIGHT 2008

I wish to give a big thanks to all K-4 students for providing the material in this book. Their quotes have inspired much laughter and discussion at formal dinners, cocktail parties, family gatherings and especially our own dinner table. I thank them for the "Funny Phonics" which shed light on the complexities of the English language, the "X-Rated" comments that made me shutter, the "Zingers" that made my day, the "Understanding Anatomy" comments that made me blush and the "9/11" comments that brought tears to my eyes.

Mrs. Maxwell, "the other teacher" and my Ed McMahon, deserves a huge thanks. Her unpublished job description has no boundaries. She has been the sentinel and "sensorer" of the class room comments. My "Famous Quotations" were all recorded and edited by her. Also, thanks to my family, Roger, Erica and LeeAnn for encouraging me to publish the quotes and for providing their editorial and technological skills.

Cindy Boerma

Through the past ten years, I have laughed, cried and sometimes cringed over comments that have been voiced by the precious children in my charge. They have amazed me day in and day out with their actions, views and insights into their little world. Mrs. Robertson and I recorded these quips with a glint and sometimes a tear in our eye.

Many times my daughters, Madison and M.E., have listened intently as I recounted the days' events, mostly because this joy that I received from my students had to be shared with others.
I offer my humble thanks to all of the children I have taught, because I would not be the mother, the teacher and the person I am today had it not been for them. These children have shown me unconditional love and allowed me to look at life again through the innocent eyes of a four year old.

Deena Eberhardt

# ABOUT THE COVER ARTIST

Danielle Marie Fox is the daughter of Richard and Jill Fox. She grew up in Athens, Georgia. After graduating from Cedar Shoals High School, she attended the University of Pittsburgh and Savannah College of Art and Design where she received her B.F.A. in Graphic Design.

Danielle is a freelance graphic artist and also works for Silverander Communications – a graphic design agency located in Santa Barbara, California, with clients located across the nation. She resides in Ojai, California, with her boyfriend, Eric, and their two dogs, Nico and Elwood.

You can view more of Danielle's work at www.creativehotlist.com/dfox.

# CONTENTS

| | | |
|---|---|---|
| A | ............... | All About Animals |
| B | ............... | Birds and the Bees |
| C | ............... | Conclusions |
| D | ............... | Dads |
| E | ............... | Explanations |
| F | ............... | Funny Phonics |
| G | ............... | God |
| H | ............... | Honesty |
| I | ............... | Inquisitiveness |
| J | ............... | Juvenile Jabbering |
| K | ............... | Keen Quips |
| L | ............... | Life and Death |
| M | ............... | Moms |
| N | ............... | 9/11 |
| O | ............... | Opinions |
| P | ............... | Perceptions |
| Q | ............... | Questions |
| R | ............... | Reality |
| S | ............... | Sickness and Health |
| T | ............... | Truthfulness |
| U | ............... | Understanding Anatomy |
| V | ............... | Verbal Views |
| W | ............... | Wisdom |
| X | ............... | X-Rated |
| Y | ............... | Young Ideas |
| Z | ............... | Zingers |

# - A -
# All About Animals

"I know the biggest animal in space, a cow because he jumps over the moon."

"What are baby rabbits called?"
"Rabblets!"

"My aunt has a cow, and it had baby pigs."

"Did you know pigs have pepperonis in them?"

"Vultures, they eat dead animals. I bet they get confused when animals are sleeping."

"My momma said you get ham from a pig's butt."

"I'm not allergic to milk, but I am allergic to bugs, sharks and killer whales."

After Mrs. Eberhardt gave each child a peacock feather, one child shrugged and said, "I guess she just left him naked."

"Mrs. Eberhardt, do you think bees go to heaven after they sting you?"

"This is not a wild animal. It's my pet turtle. It's got lots of germs, and it poops in its' water?"

"Do you think chickens know we like to eat them?"

"My dog doesn't have his dangles anymore, so he can't make babies."

"Can birds fly backwards? No, they do U-turns like my mom.

# - B -
# Birds and the Bees

"I'm going to Disney World in one day, and we're starting on a baby."

"I know someone who's about pregnant."

"Babies come out of girls. What if a baby was inside a boy?"
"Wow! That would be something!"

"First you have to get married. Then go on a honeymoon, and then you have kids."
"First you go on a date, come home and rest a little. When you're resting you talk about how kids are, then go back to the hospital and get some kids."

"We're going to Atlanta to our friends to watch them get pregnant... they are going to pour water over the baby's head."

"When I was in my mom's tummy, I did gymnastics."

"Mrs. Boerma, I have a baby in my mom's tummy."

"When you get married you do it and get babies in your tummy — only girls get babies. There's a seed in a girl's stomach when she's small. The babies get out somehow, maybe out of your belly button."
"That's called a C-section."

"Mrs. Boerma, I'm never going to get married — never, never!"
"Why not?"
"Because I don't ever want to have kids."
"It's one big hurt to cut a baby out of your tummy."

# - C -
# Conclusions

"I need some new pants, these stay in my bottom."

"You're an old teacher."
"You mean I have been teaching a long time?"
"No, you're old – you have spots on your hands!"

"I know how to cooperate."
"How so?"
"In picking out my new clothes, in the dressing room, I pretended to like the clothes she was picking out. I cooperated with my mom."

"What number comes after 39? Thirty ten?"

"I don't know that letter. It's not in my name anyway."

"If I drink Coke my tummy thunders."

"We still have our Christmas tree. It will be alive forever, because it's fake."

"My mom said Mr. Urich said I can't bring my umbrella to school. Does he want me to 'drown'd'?"

"Girls can be dentists, girls can be doctors, but girls can't take their shirts off outside."

"I think her brain is dead, 'cause she's not thinking real well."

# - D -
# Dads

"My dad can spell bad words."

"Did you know George Bush, George W. Bush is a liar? That's what my dad says."

"My dad killed a decoy once."

"My dad's a doctor, but he works at the house, too. I help him. He changes light bulbs, answers the phone, fixes the curtains when they come off the porch. He just does lots."

"My dad seems sad today. I don't know what's wrong. It might be because of his hair going away."

"What does your dad do?"
"He washes the dishes, does the laundry and goes to work to make money. He goes to an office where the phones ring, and he answers them. I think he's called a lawyer."

"I have a bumble bee dress, but my fanny shows, and my daddy won't let me wear it."

"We have two black labs, one is little and she digs in our backyard. My dad wants to kill her or give her away."

"Yesterday we got in an accident. Dad stinks at driving. He says a lot of bad words when he crashes."

"You did a good job doing your self portrait, but you forgot your pants."
"That means I was naked. Did you know my dad sleeps naked?"

"My mom is smarter than my dad."
"How do you know?"
"My mom told me."
"What does you dad say?"
"He says she's right!"

"The government takes all your money. I heard it on the radio in my dad's truck."

"Boy, parents are sometimes fat! My dad is fat."

"Daddy promised we would go tonight, but momma says he sometimes stretches the truth. How far will it stretch?"


"Where are your knuckles?"
"Right here (made a fist). My daddy says I can't hit at school, but anyplace else somebody hits me he says to punch them back. Just flatten them, but not at school, that's what my daddy says!"


"He's like my dad, he has hair, but he is kinda bald."

"We're going to nana's. Daddy is not, 'cause he says she makes him lose his 'tempers'. I don't know how, 'cause her house is little."

"Did only our mom's make us?"
"No, your dad made you too."
"God made us."
"What about dad?"
"He watches us when mom is at the grocery store."
"What else do dads do?"
"Go to work and make money!"

# - E -
# Explanations

"If I didn't go to school my mom says I would not be able to get married and take care of my family. I don't really want to get married."

"I'm not half white, I'm half Indian and half Pilgrim, because my great, great, great-grandmother was an Indian."

"Frozen is a more sophisticated word than freeze."

"My one grandpa divorced and went to another one."

"Someone in Good Housekeeping in the back is tooting on us."
"Tooting? What does tooting mean?"
"You know, it's bathroom stuff."
"What were you doing in Good Housekeeping?"
"Well, I was playing with the stuffed praying mantis, and he, the praying mantis, had real bad gases, and since he, the praying mantis, is not real, I had to make both the noise and the smell for him."

"Those guys just keep believing there are witches, but – but- witches live in haunted houses and haunted houses aren't real, so witches aren't real."

"Mrs. Boerma, I'm mad at the rain."
"Why?"
"Because it makes me get all wet."
"But the plants and animals need the water."
"Just use the watering can."
"What about the trees?"
"You should water the roots of the tree with the watering can too."

# - F -
# Funny Phonics

"Careful Mrs. Eberhardt, that 'spearment' might 'splode' on you!"

"Can I 'unbackwards' my t-shirt, 'cause I thought it was 'rightwards'."

"Dinosaurs live in Australia, and they are 'unstinct'."

"I got a 'speedo' bite."

"If you get close to a dinosaur, you might can smell them, and that's why they're called 'exstinct'."

"I know how to 'tribble' a basketball."

"It's a 'reptangle'."

"An octagon has eight sides, just like an octopus with eight legs. The only difference is one is a 'gon', and one is a 'pus'."

"I 'weared hear' muffs."

"Can I 'un-rase' the board?"

"He said my hair is 'ex-static'!"

"My mom and dad says Clinton is not doing too good at his work. They think he might get 'in peaches'."

"Volcanoes ooze 'saliva'."

"Our state bird is the Brown 'Flasher'."

"Me and my friend..."
"Wait, who is 'meand'? Try my friend and I."
"Mrs. Boerma, I listened at my house last night, and we have a 'meand' there. In fact, we have a lot of 'meands'. Do you think I need to tell my mom and dad there are no 'meands'?"

"My mom and dad says Clinton is not doing too good at his job! They wish he could get 'impecked'."

"I'm staying for 'expended' day."

"I'm staying in 'extensive' day today."

"I'm staying in 'intensive' day today."

"My throat has been 'strepped'."

"We get the milk from the cow by the 'gutter'."

"I'm going to be the flower girl, and my brother will be the ring 'master' at the wedding."

"The cow's milk shoots out its' 'putter'."

"Mrs. Eberhardt, my mosquito bite 'switches'."

"I had a baby cavity in my tooth, and I had to get a 'refilling' in it."

# - G -
# God

"God was the first man on the moon."
"No, Neil Armstrong was the first man on the moon. My dad told me that."

"Mr. Urich is the tallest man in the world."
"No, God is."

"God is always right. He never makes a mistake."

"Do you know why flamingos are pink?"
"I dunno, I guess God made them that way."

"It was supposed to rain yesterday, not today. It didn't rain yesterday, and it is raining today. I guess God changed his mind."

"God made a lot of things, heaven and our earth."
"Don't forget God made our poop stink too."

"There has to be an end because there's heaven."
"But heaven is after space."
"Heaven is higher than infinity."

"God must be mad at us because it won't stop raining for us to go outside."

"What is evaporation?"
"Water goes back up so God can use it again for another rain shower."

"We can fly when we die, when we get wings in heaven."

"I don't know if the school wants to hear this or not, but listen to me, there is a part in the Bible called 'doo-doo dooteronimous'."

"How does day and night work?"
"God does it. He was lonely making the whole world. He needed light to work, found He needed more people and needed a sun and moon, 'cause nobody could see so well."

"When people die you have to bury them. And you have to bury them in your front yard, or God won't take them to heaven."

"If you do good things you go to heaven. If you do bad things you go to hell."
"I certainly don't believe in hell. The devil can go into your heart and make you do bad things. I don't believe there is pitch forks down there."
"A preacher is a guy who lives in a church and tells you what is good and bad."

"If you are in heaven you're going to love it – you're alive. You're going to fly in heaven with God. There will be no cemeteries, and no one will ever die. There's no place you can get out of the world, because the whole place is the world."

"Which church do you go to?"
"I don't know – oh – it's the one where you learn about Jesus."

# - H -
# Honesty

"We don't wear pajamas at my house!"

"Is your daddy your coach too?"
"No, he just stands on the side and pretends."

"My mom said she cooked that snack, but she really bought it at Kroger."

"I hit 420 homeruns yesterday."

"I don't wear PJ's. Really nobody in my family wears them."

"Do you hope for a girl or a boy baby?"
"I really wanted a puppy."

"My baby sister is almost as gorgeous as I was."

"My mom is bringing ducks, but she's not here yet. She's got to put her clothes on first, before she comes."

"He shoved and pushed me down!"
"I shoved him because he shoved me first. I wanted to show him what it felt like."

"My pretend sister was in the play we saw this morning."

"I've never seen anyone bake a cake before! We usually buy them at the store."

"I'm getting on my nerves."

# - I -
# Inquisitiveness

"If I walk backwards, does that mean I will never get there?"

"If somebody is not here today to sign the thank you card, do we just skip him?"

"Mrs. Eberhardt, do you think amphibians have to go to school too?"

"We're going to a special assembly this morning, and I want to tell you about it."
"Yes, I know someone died."
"Jesus died, too."
"This is a memorial assembly for Mr. John Wilkins."
"Yes, it's the man that started Athens Academy."
"Everybody dies sometime."
"Was he old?"
"Did he get sick?"
"My dog Sampson died, he fell down."
"Austin our dog died, it made my mom and dad sad."
"My hamster died on Easter, it was Fred. It was little not old."
"My nana is going to talk in there."
"Will he, uh, Mr. Wilson, I mean, Mr. Wilkins, will he be arose again like Jesus?"

"Mrs. Eberhardt, is boob a bad word?"

"What if the butterfly went backwards and ended up an egg?

"Is today tomorrow?"

ABC

# - J -
# Juvenile Jabbering

"My grandmother makes stone soup, but without the stones."

"He bit me! Tell him it's not snack time!"

"Mrs. Boerma is a wizard, and Mrs. Maxwell is a miracle."

At snack time we made Jello Jigglers and heard this comment – "GOD, these are good!!!!!"

"George Washington married Barbara Bush."

"No, I don't have sisters! I have two daughters."

"My mom is usually a terrible cook. She puts salt on the vegetables instead of sugar."

"I like to drink apple juice, but it burns coming out."

"I have a ghost in the show and tell bag. Well, not a real one, just pretend."

"I know how to make a lower case 4."

# - K -
# Keen Quips

"I don't ever want to get married. I want to be a kid forever!"

"I don't think I care for pickles." (takes a taste) "I'm sure now."

"I think this shoe is too untied."

"I don't know how to count to 20, but I can count to 100."

"Mrs. Boerma, did you tell my mom at the conference that I was smart?"
"Yes, I did."
"Whew!!! That's good, 'cause I really am really smart."

"Mrs. Eberhardt, I brushed my teeth this morning. Smell them."

"These came out of my nose! They are magnets and they start with M."

"My sister blows bubbles in the tub." (child points to bottom)

"Mrs. Eberhardt my heart is chirping."

"Mrs. Boerma, do you know why I checked out a science book? Because I already know all my math, and it's incredible."

# - L -
# Life and Death

"My aunt died once, she just died one time."

"Two things that are really sad and bad – my dad's friend's dad died, and my dad's dad died."
"Oh, that's too bad – had he been sick?"
"Yeah, a long time. Well, he had to have two toes cut off."
"OOOOOH – did he have diabetes?"
"No, he just had bad toes."

"It's still dead, 'cause it hasn't come back alive."

"A fire could make you die bad."

"One time I jumped in the swimming pool when it was hot, and drowned, but just once."

"I've been to my dad's mom and dad's house. Their old house was in Maine."
"Did they move?"
"No, they can't move – they're dead."

"I had three cats, but now I have two. One got sick and had to take medicine, but kept spitting it out. So, then he had to get shots in the doctor's office. Now he is just dead in the woods!"

"My brother, he killed a dead bee."

"I have an insect in a jar – oh – it's kinda dead – it looks like it was trying to get to the water and just didn't make it – it'll be ok."

# - M -
# Moms

"My mom thinks she's going to give my sister to the school next year."

"My mom's birthday is today. She's 40!!!!! That's not 40 pounds, that's 40 old."

"My mom knows everything."
"No, God knows everything."
"Well then, my mom and God knows everything."

"My mom is not going to understand this – not one bit – she wants me to do better than this."

"My mom stays home to take of us in the house. She has an important job."

"This picture of my mom is where her hair is blowing in the wind, but it doesn't look too windy. Maybe it's just her hair."

"Jewish children get a gift everyday for 8 days. Wow! If my mom knew that, it would be great."

"My mommy says my daddy snores. The nose strips don't work."

"My mommy says my brother is a slave at our house."

"See this dimple on my cheek? My mom has one on her bottom just like it."

"My mom sneezes in Spanish."

"Guess what? My mom got a piece of paper from the policeman yesterday. She put it in her pocketbook and said not to tell daddy."

"Please move your clothespin to red."
"I can't. My mom said I can't get on red anymore."
"Please move you clothespin and think about what you need to do to keep off red."
"My mom just said this morning, 'Don't let Mrs. Boerma have to put you on red today.' So I can't move my clothespin to red."
"Please move it now."
"Ok, ok I will, but my mom is going to be really mad at you, 'cause she said I just couldn't let Mrs. Boerma put me on red again. Do you really want her mad at you?"
"I can handle it. I'll talk to her."
"Ok, maybe she'll understand."

"Spring Break – one thing I did that wasn't very much fun – I cleaned up my house. My mom thinks it's very much fun – but I don't see it."

"Sometimes my mom says cuss words. Sometimes my dad does, too – real bad ones!!!!"

"What do you think your mom is doing?"
"Probably just sitting on the couch, eating Bon-Bons!"

"We missed you. Were you sick?"
"No, I just didn't want to come to school. I wanted to help my mom do the laundry."
"Do you like school?"
"Yes, sure – but I like my mom better, and I wanted to spend time with her."

"My mom is half cat – she eats tuna for lunch, dinner but not breakfast."

"I've seen a roach before. It was in my kitchen, and mommy said not to tell anyone."

"What is your mom's first name?"
"She hasn't told me yet."

"You always make us cut things! You're even meaner than my mom!"

"My mom grounded me and my sister for something I don't understand, but she did it anyway!"

"At home my mom is the boss of us! She tells all of us what to do. Even my dad!!! Once he was talking and talking, and she told him to be quiet, and he did."
"Well, my dad is the boss at our house, 'cause he's the biggest."

"Money and work – my mom doesn't know how to do that."

"My mom is real sick. She had to spend the night in the bathroom."

"Mrs. Maxwell, sometimes I feel nervous about being at school."
"Why?"
"Because my mom is not here."
"But she's usually not at school."
"I mean when she's out of town."
"Well, when you feel nervous you just tell Mrs. Boerma and me, and we'll love on you some extra."
"Ok! That's a deal."

"I've never heard of that animal that starts with an M. I've heard of a martini. My mom drinks it. I think it has lemons in it, I think, no, maybe strawberries. Poison I think."

# - N -
# 9/11

    September 12, 2001, was a humbling day in our teaching career. We spoke our normal morning greetings, and then just listened and recorded the comments these small children made to each other describing the horrific previous day.

"They, bad guys, went through a building. The plane exploded – the people died."

"The bad people broke the building in New York and Washington, D.C. George Bush is very mad. I'm very sad."

"The building fell down because these planes – very powerful planes – knocked them down. President Bush in Washington is very mad at the bad guys. He needs to throw them away. Maybe under a dump truck. We need to use kind language, but my dad, he doesn't know how, but I 'teached' him."

"The building fell down, because the bad guys ran into it. George Bush is mad about it, because he wants it safe in Georgia and other places. I think we should kill them. I think 'Georgia' Bush will get the Army to do it."

"The plane crashed into the city, because the bad guys are bad guys. We should help them build back up the city and bring the bad guys to the president with handcuffs – then put them in jail – throw keys in the trash."

"Some people got killed because New York got attacked by bad guys. God is taking care of it. George Bush and an angel are taking care of it – Our Lord. We should pray for all the people who were hurt or killed. We should kill the bad guys. My dad might use his hunting guns."

"The airplane crashed. The mean man came up and shot the captain. The building fell down into a hundred blocks – people 50 to 100 and 2 died. George Bush was not in that building. He's looking for somebody. He's sending a real army – like a tank army to get him. My dad gave money to help people in the fall down building."

"Sadam Hussein is the bad president. Children die if they don't do what he says. George W. Bush is the good president."

"Sadam Hussein is not a president! He is a king."

"We have more bombs than they do. He's not going to come here. If the good guys see him flying here with bombs, they will shoot them and make them blow up."

"He has weapons to kill lots of people hidden, and they aren't supposed to tell, or they will be killed."

"Fire fighters had to work all night, because the building fell down."

"Granny was to come yesterday, but couldn't because a terrible thing happened."

"Some guards in New York are not to let anymore bad people come."
"They snuck up and planned to do it."
"That was all there was on t.v. I couldn't watch anything."
"The president is mad! Our President 'Georgia' Bush."

   A month later...
"Airplanes crashed into the World Trade Center – terrorists did it – we should find them and kill them – the Army will take care of it."

"The bad guys destroyed their home. We are mad at him. I think it is sad to see 'Georgia' Bush's planet crash."

"A plane ran into a building – bad guys were driving it. The people in the back and in the building are all killed. President Bush is going to kill the bad guys."

"It's bad. An airplane crashed into the buildings – bad guys did it. We're making money for the people that died and the firemen. President Bush is the boss of everybody. He'll decide if we should decide if we'll have WWII. It's pretty sad. My mom and dad are pretty sad and mad. It's a way bad idea to run into a building. You should curve the plane."

"What is a five-sided shape called?"
"A pentagon."
"Like the building in Washington, D.C. blown up by the Taliban."
"My dad said we'd killed almost all of them by bombs."
"That bad guy – our team is trying to get him."
"The Air Force is my favorite. I'm going to be in the Air Force when I grow up."
"He's hiding in a cave, but we can't quite find him. We're fighting in the other country."
"Our military uses things to fight – swords, planes, guns, submarines, bombs and cannons."
"When we defend ourselves, we are fighting for our country."
"Hope."
"Love."
"Peace."

# - O -
# Opinions

"The biggest, largest one in our school is Mr. Chambers."
"No, the biggest is Mr. Urich."
"No, he's the biggest, tallest but not the most important. Mr. C. is the most important."
"Do you know the biggest, most important in the whole wide world? It's in this order – God, Jesus Christ, my sister and Santa Claus!!!"

"We're having a drought. That means we're getting drops instead of just rain."

"My mom and dad are being ugly today."

"When you're 50 you can go to college. I'm not going to high school or college – it's too hard. But I have to ask my mom."

"You have it all wrong Mrs. Boerma, my name doesn't even have a lower case in it."

"How was your day at school?"
"Well, not so good."
"The toilet wouldn't flush. The water didn't work at all, and I think they're making a barn out of our playground, 'cause it's covered in hay."

"This is the most 'specialist' day!"

"We don't want to get 'telled' on in this class."

"If I put a tissue over my finger before I put it in my nose, it don't work right."

"Can you think of a liquid?"
"Something that tastes good to moms, but not to children – like beer."

"They write chalk the places people get dead."

"I threw up three times in Colorado. It was just too cold."

"A tub is used to keep CapriSuns, beers and Cokes in."

2000 election …
"'Georgia' W. Bush is from Georgia."
"No, he's not, he's from Texas. I know that for sure."
"Nope, his momma never would have named him Georgia if he was from Texas."

"'Georgia' Bush kinda is winning, and Al Gore is still crying and acting like a baby. You can't cry in war."

"Al Gore is doing whining, because he wants to win. George Bush is being happy – that's why he's winning."

"George Bush is winning, but he hasn't won yet."

"Bush is going to be president, because Al Gore is cheating, because he wants to be president. He wants to win."

"George Bush was winning more, because he wasn't cheating a bit, and Al Gore was cheating."

"Cheating is like when you're running, and you take a short cut."

"Concede means you lost, and I won."
"Concede means to give up."
"We saw George Bush on t.v. He was in one of those cars – they were taking him to be president."

# - P -
# Perceptions

"Good morning – Where were you?"
"Where I was."

"I have one brother. He's one. He turned one about five years ago."

"I'm taking swimming lessons today." I don't know why I'm fine with my floaties."

"My mom and dad have been married for 89 years."

"You gotta get over May before you can get on June."

"I'm going to spend the night with my grandmother for 7 days."

"The Indians have arrow guns."

"Kids are almost intelligent. Adults are really intelligent."

"What kind of donut is your favorite?"
"The kind with frosting on it."
"What kind of frosting."
"The kind on top of the donut."

"My grandparents live on the other side of the world in Colorado."

"The movers picked up our stuff yesterday. I hope we get it back."

# - Q -
# Questions

"What are you doing with a tissue in your ear?"
"I have booger in my ear."

"What is a mud pie anyway?"

"What's a record? Is it the same as a CD?"

"Mrs. Eberhardt, are you sure my taste buds are growing?"

"How many more years do we have to go to school before school is over?"

"Do you think ants know they're short?"

"Mrs. Boerma, how do you know all these lessons and letters? Did you go to school and listen to your teacher instead of your mother?"

"What is talking back?"
"That means repeat after me?"

"Were we born on our birthday?"

"When is tomorrow?"

"What do you get when a boy kisses a girl?"
"Just germs!!"

"If Bubbles (classroom fish) gets sick does her mommy come back from the ocean to take care of her?"

# - R -
# Reality

"Mrs. Eberhardt, your legs are prickly."

"I'm having a bad day."
"What does a bad day mean?"
"A bad day means it's not so good."

"Mrs. Eberhardt, your doll's leg is broken. She needs insurance."

"Mrs. Boerma, you are wrong! You didn't see me driving to school this morning. That was my mom. I can't drive yet."

"Sometimes if I spin real fast, I tip over."

"Do you know when my dad's coming home? He's coming in February."
"That's cool."
"No, it's not cool. It's long!"

"Mrs. Eberhardt, I splattered in my pants."

"Were you sick yesterday?"
"No, I had an attitude and so, I couldn't come to school. I was mad and wouldn't get in my dad's car. So, that's why I didn't get to come to school."

"I can never do what I want!"
"Get used to it - - that's real life."
"Then I sure don't like real life!"

"My grandma smells like cheese!"

# - S -
# Sickness and Health

"I kinda broke my finger, but it's ok now. They sewed it back on."

"I was sick yesterday. I was sneezing and coughing, a little fever, no diarrhea, but some cavities."

"I think my head might be hurting. Can I get a BandAid for that?"

"I'm going to have surgery. The kind where they pull something out of my nose or throat."

"I got chicken pox when I ate chicken legs."

"I really don't want to clean up right now. I'm getting a little disease."

"I had this really humongous, bad cold – the kind when you blow the boogers just automatically fly into the tissue. I'm going to the dentist today. Talking about my boogers made me think about my teeth needing cleaning."

"My throat is coughing me."

"I have drainage problems."

"I am going to wash my hands a lot today. Everybody has been with the virus, either throwing up or having diarrhea, and I'm not going to get sick. We have lost three babies at our house, and we're not going to lose this one!"

"When you are ill the doctor takes the ill out of you."

# - T -
# Truthfulness

"Why do we need a change of clothes at school?"
"In case you have an accident."
"Don't you trust us?"

"Your class is pretty cool. It's got pretty cool stuff! I might just like it enough to come almost every day."

"Cute shoes!"
"Cute, but they don't fit!"

"Mrs. Eberhardt, I tried to make my bed, but my maid doesn't like me to."

"Please put your thinker cap on and tie it in a triple bow."
"Sorry, but I don't know how to tie."

"I love cake, but it doesn't love me." (points to tummy)

"I brushed my teeth two times this time – morning and night."
"Thank goodness, now your breath won't smell when I come to your house!"

"What was your favorite thing about school?"
"I loved playing and learning – learning and playing."
"I love to play and work – our practice here makes perfect."
"This grade has a great playground and good work."
"Learning my letters, and I liked my teacher, I loved my teachers, they're great."
"I loved it all – circle time, our play – learning about America and painting."
"I loved learning my numbers. I already knew all my letters – just knew them forever."
"I like the work. I like to do things. Practice makes perfect."

# - U -
# Understanding Anatomy

"If you take your appendix out, you can't have babies."

"My mom won't be in the car pool line today. She is at the doctors. You remember when she got stitched up so the baby wouldn't fall out? Well, the stitches fell out and the baby is fixin' to fall out again. They will just stitch her up again. Then it can't fall out again!"

"If we put a bellybutton on the bear, do we need to put bosoms on it?"

"Whenever we talk about body parts, I think about not scratching a mosquito bite, because all my parts might come out."

"Did you know that under your nipples, if you push in you can feel your carcass?"

"Mrs. Eberhardt, I swallowed a penny yesterday. I had an x-ray, and it's right here. I have to watch my poop now."

"Do you know what nipples are? They are like boobs. Moms have them. Dad has boobs, too. They're smaller than moms. I have nipples, not boobs. Only ladies have boobs."

"Mrs. Eberhardt, do you know what a penis is?"

"Mrs. Boerma, check out my knees. I dropped my 'hiney' off my swing and 'stumped' my knees."

# - V -
# Verbal Views

"They used to think the Earth was flat. Now they say it's round."
"I don't know, but it's pretty flat at my house."

"Who is the vice-president of the United States?"
"I think, let me see, I know, it's Rush Limbaugh."

"I was named after my aunt, and my dad was named after me!"

"To get a driver's license you go to SAM'S and have your picture taken, and they put it in a license for you."

"That's a picture of the Kentucky Fried Chicken guy." (picture of George Washington)

"If the tooth fairy dips the wing in the water and it turns blue, it means the fairy is a boy. If it turns pink, it's a girl, and if it turns purple it means the fairy is both a boy and a girl. That's what my dad said."

"Do you think we'll have an earthquake?"
"No, we have grass that holds everything together!"

"That's the Virgin Mary!" (picture of Mona Lisa)

"She pulled the tub away from me and said she was going to poke my eyes out! I don't want to sit down and talk about her being my friend. I just don't want her to poke my eyes out! She thinks after this day I will forget it and be friends again. She don't know that I will forget – I don't forget. And I don't want to hear a bit out of her mouth again!

# - W -
# Wisdom

"At the beach, the sun went down into the water when it set."

"What do all plants need in order to live?"
"Air, milk and goldfish."

"All the letters in my name are in the alphabet!"

"Mrs. Boerma, you are smarter than the SmartBoard!"

"Three sleeps and it's my birthday."

"My grandmother says that pretty is as pretty does!"

"Mr. Chambers is going to read to us today. Who is he?"
"He's in charge of the programs for the play."
"He is the president of Athens Academy."
"He makes the rules and consequences for the school."
"He is a very busy man."
"I think he is James's granddad."
"He works for the school so it can be a good school and does things for the children – good things, he works hard."

"I have been practicing it a lot and getting it straight in my brain."

"I am five and three quarters today."

"Today I am five and a fourth."

"What does this (Q) look like?
"That looks like an O with a leg."

# - X -
# X-Rated

"We were throwing stink bombs."
"What are stink bombs?"
"They are like – a – like farts – you know."

"My momma said that white cardboard thing with a string in her purse is not a special candle."

"I hate sleeping with my brother. He dreams he's on the potty."

"Excuse me please, I farted.
"But we don't say that word!"
"But, I did! And a fart is a fart!"

"Please give me an F word."
" F & # %."
"Hmmm, I don't think I know how to spell that word."
"Yes you do Mrs. Boerma. Just sound it out like this – ffff, &&&&, ####, %%%%."
"I think we need to go on to math, it's getting late."

"Know what piss means?"
"Yeah, it's a bathroom word – it means tee-tee."

"I just pooted."
"Say, excuse me."
"Excuse me, I just pooted."

"Please give me an F word."
" F & # %."
"What did you say?"
" F & # %."
"Whoa, where did you hear that?"
"My dad says it all the time!"

# - Y -
# Young Ideas

"When you grow up, you get married, have children, build a house, and sometimes you have to think about getting a new wife."

"He broke my feelings."

"I don't want to go to kindergarten. They want me to get big."

"The pilgrims are little people that wore cowboy hats and all these brown clothes with buttons. They came from India."

"My baby is coming tomorrow, and I want it to be a boy or girl."

"My shoelaces are not good at being tied."

"Why are you afraid of the dark?"
"It might bite me."

"Mr. Urich is so lucky. He gets the playground all to himself when we go home."

"Freckles just 'growed' on me."

"I wish I had eyes in the back of my head like Mrs. Eberhardt."

"My mom keeps packing me ham sandwiches for lunch. She must think I love them."

"My grandma is picking me up today, because my mom and dad are going on a second honeymoon. The first one didn't work out so well."

# - Z -
# Zingers

"It's Valentine's Day so, go home and give your mom and dad a kiss."
"Shouldn't we do that everyday?"

"Would you please put that on my desk?"
"Do you think I'm the maid?"

"In Maine, at the old blue house, I wake up and pee on the house."
"My dad pees off the porch."
"Me and my dad pee off the porch too."
"My dad and I can pee anywhere we want to!"

"I have a rock to show today."
"It looks like a rock, but it's soft!"
"Yes, I know, it's a broken rock."
"It smells bad, too!"
"I know, that's why I have it in a plastic bag."
"Are you sure it's a rock?"
"No, actually I think it's putty."
(Actually it was a frozen dog dropping!)

"Please don't talk to your neighbor during circle time."
"He's not my neighbor. He doesn't live any where near me."

"You may go play now, but try to play with someone you won't have trouble with."
"How about it if I just pretend somebody's there playing with me?"

"Why do we have to have conference day? I really don't think it's any of momma's business."

# Thanks to the K-4 Classes from:

1989-1990
1990-1991
1991-1992
1992-1993
1993-1994
1994-1995
1995-1996
1996-1997
1997-1998
1998-1999
1999-2000
2000-2001
2001-2002
2002-2003
2003-2004
2004-2005
2005-2006
2006-2007
2007-2008

Made in the USA
Columbia, SC
03 April 2025